KNOW IT ALL!

TECHNOLOGY

MOIRA BUTTERFIELD AND PAT JACOBS

Cavendish Square
New York

Published in 2016 by Cavendish Square Publishing, LLC
243 5th Avenue, Suite 136, New York, NY 10016

First Edition

Website: cavendishsq.com

This publication represents the opinions and views of the author based on his or her personal experience, knowledge, and research. The information in this book serves as a general guide only. The author and publisher have used their best efforts in preparing this book and disclaim liability rising directly or indirectly from the use and application of this book.

CPSIA Compliance Information: Batch #CW16CSQ

All websites were available and accurate when this book was sent to press.

Cataloging-in-Publication Data

Butterfield, Moira.
Technology / by Moira Butterfield and Pat Jacobs.
p. cm. — (Know it all)
Includes index.
ISBN 978-1-5026-0904-5 (hardcover) ISBN 978-1-5026-0902-1 (paperback) ISBN 978-1-5026-0905-2 (ebook)
1. Technology — Juvenile literature. I. Butterfield, Moira, 1960-. II. Title.
T48.B88 2016
600—d23

Project managed and commissioned by Dynamo Limited
Consultants: Sally Morgan, Dr. Patricia Macnair, Brian Williams, Carey Scott, Dr. Mike Goldsmith.
Authors: Moira Butterfield and Pat Jacobs
Editor / Picture Researcher: Dynamo Limited
Design: Dynamo Limited

KEY – tl top left, tc top center, tr top right, cl center left, c center, cr center right, bl bottom left, bc bottom center, br bottom right.
All photographs and illustrations in this book © Shutterstock except: Volodymyr Krasyuk/Shutterstock.com, cover; Corbis 12tl TOBIAS SCHWARZ/Reuters; GODD.com (Markus Junker, Rolf Schröter, Patrick Tilp) 4t, 6t; iStockphoto.com 13tr, 25tr; Malcolm Goodwin/Moonrunner Design 4b, 13l, 14, 16l, 27b.

Printed in the United States of America

Table of Contents

Connecting the World............................ 4

Computers Today 6

Computers Tomorrow 7

Artificial Intelligence 8

Robotics 9

High-Tech Homes 10

The Sky's the Limit 11

Hitting the Highway 12

Going Green 13

Flying Without Wings 14

Flying by Wire 16

Cruising at the Edge of Space 17

Nanotechnology 18

Nanomaterials 19

Generating Electricity 20

Renewable Energy 21

Biotechnology 22

Genetic Engineering 23

Future Foods 24

Farming 25

Medicine 26

Bionic Body Parts 27

Glossary 28

Further Information 30

Index 31

Connecting the World

The Internet began in the early 1960s as a network for use by the American government, universities, and research laboratories. It became available to the public in the 1990s.

How the Internet works

If you email a message or file to a friend it is broken up into "packets" of data. When they arrive at your friend's computer, they are pieced back together, like a puzzle. For small files, this journey takes just a few seconds.

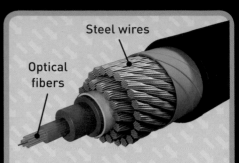

Steel wires

Optical fibers

An underwater web

Undersea fiber-optic cables crisscross the globe, linking your computer to those on other continents. If one is damaged—by being hit by a ship's anchor, for example—Internet traffic is redirected along a different route.

Each packet carries your friend's IP (Internet protocol) address.

Packets are directed by routers along one of thousands of paths.

IP: 221.77 50.155

Sometimes, all the packets take the same route; at other times, each one goes a different way.

The Digital Revolution

Twenty years ago hardly anyone had heard of the Internet, yet now it has totally changed our lives.

⬆ Social networking

About a third of the world's population uses the Internet—which is about 2.27 billion people. Each day, they send 267.4 billion email messages and make 2.85 billion Google searches. Facebook has 845 million active users, who upload 250 million photos a day, while 465 million people use Twitter and send up to 175 million tweets every day.

⬇ Keeping in touch

We can make free face-to-face calls to friends and family all over the world using a computer with a webcam.

⬆ On the move

Superfast smartphones offer a better Internet service than many home computers, and apps add even more functions, ranging from a guitar tuner to games. When smartphones scan QR codes (a type of barcode) they are automatically connected to a website.

⬆ Up in the cloud

When you log on to Facebook, you are using cloud computing. Facebook stores sixty billion photos which are kept "in the cloud." The cloud is actually a very large number of computers, of many types and sizes, which are located all over the world.

💡 Know it all!

● The World Wide Web is not the same as the Internet. The Internet is a huge network that links computers all over the world. The World Wide Web is the collection of linked pages that can be accessed while using the Internet.

● English physicist Sir Tim Berners-Lee invented the Web in 1989, with the help of Belgian computer scientist Robert Cailliau.

● A website address is known as a URL, which stands for uniform resource locater.

Computers Today

When the first computers went on sale in the early 1950s they cost more than $1 million each—the same as about $9 million today. Instead of modern microscopic transistors, they used valves the size of lightbulbs and were so big that they filled a whole room.

OLED (organic light-emitting diode) screens are ultra thin. The display is very bright and does not use much power.

The touch pad senses the position of the user's finger.

Central processing unit

The hard drive stores data on one or more spinning aluminium or glass discs coated with magnetic recording material.

Laptops are powered by rechargeable batteries that can last for up to eight hours.

The optical disc drive uses laser light to read CDs, DVDs or Blu-ray discs.

Motherboard

Keyboard

An optical mouse uses an LED to detect movement across a surface.

Computing on the go

Today's laptops and tablets are thousands of times more powerful than the first computers. The brain of a modern computer is called the central processing unit (CPU). The CPU and the computer's memory form part of the motherboard—the computer's main printed circuit board.

Silicon chips

Computers contain different kinds of chips that are placed on printed circuit boards. Some are used for doing large calculations. Others contain memory. Each chip holds millions of transistors (electronic switches) and components that are "printed" onto a wafer of silicon.

💡 *Facts & figures*

BITS AND BYTES

1 bit is the smallest unit of data that a computer uses.

1 byte is a group of 8 bits

1 kilobyte equals 1,024 bytes

1 megabyte equals 1,024 kilobytes

1 gigabyte equals 1,024 megabytes

1 terabyte equals 1,024 gigabytes

1 petabyte equals 1,024 terabytes

1 exabyte equals 1,024 petabytes

1 zettabyte equals 1,024 exabytes

Computers Tomorrow

Some scientists believe that the age of computing has barely begun and that, in years to come, we will laugh at the size of today's laptops and tablets.

All the information held in this data center could one day be stored on a tiny microchip.

Moore's law

Moore's law is named after Gordon Moore. He predicted that the number of transistors that could be placed on a silicon chip, for the same cost, would double every eighteen to twenty-four months. This has proved to be true. Today's transistors are so small, it would take more than two thousand stacked next to each other to equal the thickness of a human hair.

Quantum leap

Nanotechnology could one day create powerful computers the size of a credit card, controlled by voice recognition software. Some experts think that, in the future, computers will be everywhere—painted onto walls and furniture or forming part of our clothes.

Squeezing more transistors onto a chip means that computers become faster and smaller.

Know it all!

● By the middle of this century, a single micro-memory card might have the same storage capacity that the whole of the Internet has today.

Brain games

Scientists predict that computers in headbands could beam data straight into our brains. If you were playing a video game, as well as seeing and hearing what was happening, you would be able to taste, smell, and feel everything, too.

⬤ Artificial Intelligence

If someone can do complicated calculations in a second or beats a grandmaster at chess, we think he or she is very intelligent. Computers can do both of these things, but they do not have the common sense of a three-year-old child.

Smart or stupid?

Computers have beaten grandmasters at chess and won quiz shows, but here are some examples of things that are easy for us, which computers would not normally know: computers cannot come up with complicated new ideas, work out what is going on in a cartoon strip, or chat like a human.

Computers can now defeat even the most skilled chess players.

Artificial intelligence will help robot rovers to explore other planets.

Artificial neural networks can warn people that a storm is coming by spotting patterns in complicated data.

Neural networks

Scientists are trying to make computers more like human brains so that they can learn, recognize patterns, and make decisions. This system is called an artificial neural network. Among other things, it can be used to forecast the weather, spot illegal bank transactions, and operate a plane's autopilot.

Exploring space

Artificial intelligence could soon be used to control spacecraft. The European Space Agency is developing control systems that can be used in robotic exploration vehicles and satellites. Space exploration missions will no longer need to be monitored by human controllers on Earth because the vehicles will be able to learn, recognize problems, carry out repairs, and make decisions themselves.

Robotics

A typical robot has a moveable arm, motors, a sensor system, a power supply, and a computer "brain." Most robots are designed to do heavy, difficult, dangerous, or boring jobs that humans do not want to do.

Snakebots

Snake robots come in many shapes and sizes. They are designed to slide into tight spaces and are especially useful in search-and-rescue operations. NASA is developing an intelligent "snakebot" that could explore other planets by slithering into cracks or climbing over rough ground where a wheeled rover would get stuck.

There is even a tiny surgical snake robot that can crawl inside the body to perform surgery.

Most industrial robots work in car factories.

Industrial robots

An industrial robot arm is similar to a human arm with a shoulder, an elbow, and a wrist. The "hand" is often a tool, such as a blowtorch, drill, or paint sprayer. Robots are more reliable and accurate than humans. They can do heavy work all day without getting tired, drill holes in exactly the same place each time, and do not stop for lunch or go on vacation.

Robot pet

Many robot pets can "see," "hear," and react to their surroundings. Some even act as guard dogs, by taking a photo of any intruders. The latest pets have artificial intelligence that allows them to learn commands and adapt their behavior in response to training.

Robot pets never shed hair or need walking.

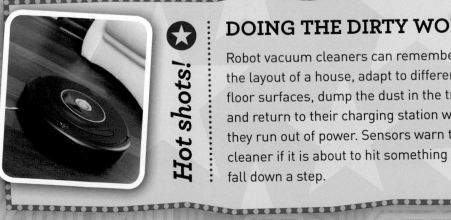

Hot shots!

DOING THE DIRTY WORK

Robot vacuum cleaners can remember the layout of a house, adapt to different floor surfaces, dump the dust in the trash and return to their charging station when they run out of power. Sensors warn the cleaner if it is about to hit something or fall down a step.

High-Tech Homes

Modern homes are getting greener and smarter. Many now generate their own electricity, have energy-saving features, and recycle water. Technology is making houses more interactive, too, with "intelligent" appliances, body-scanning door locks, and automated lighting.

Smart homes

Home automation systems use computers to control electrical devices. This might include switching the lights and television off when someone leaves a room, shading the windows in hot weather, watering plants, feeding pets, or closing the curtains when it gets dark.

Some smart fridges have a built-in dietician that tells you when you have made an unhealthy food choice.

The Heliotrope home produces five times more energy than it uses.

The pattern on the iris is unique to each person, so it is the perfect biometric key.

Forget the key

Instead of fumbling for the key, in the future we may get into our houses using just our fingers or eyes. Biometric door locks can be programmed to recognize the fingerprints or irises (the colored part of the eye) of everyone who might need to get into the house.

Clever machines

Smart appliances include washing machines that adjust the amount of water to the load, cookers that monitor the temperature of food and automatically set the cooking time, and fridges with screens that check use-by dates, suggest recipes, and send shopping lists to a smartphone.

Rotating eco house

The Heliotrope home in Germany turns to follow the sun, which powers solar panels on the roof. At the same time, the sunlight floods in through the windows and its heat is stored for use by the floor heating system. Handrails around the roof and balconies double as pipes that heat radiators and water. During hot weather, the house creates shade by turning its wooden back to the sun.

The Sky's the Limit

People have been building towers since the Middle Ages, but it was the invention of the elevator and the production of long, lightweight steel beams that made it possible to construct apartment and office blocks more than five stories high.

Fighting the wind

As skyscrapers get taller, the wind pressure on the buildings increases. The separate "tubes" of the Burj Khalifa in Dubai are designed to stop the wind from forming whirlpools that could rock the tower. Even so, it still sways backward and forward by about 6.5 feet (2 meters) at the very top.

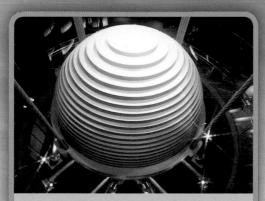

Absorbing vibrations

Between the eighty-eighth and ninety-second floors of Taiwan's Taipei 101 tower, a golden 728 ton (660 metric ton) pendulum swings back and forth, balancing the tower against the force of the wind. This system, called a tuned mass damper, is often used in skyscrapers to absorb vibrations caused by wind or earth tremors.

Know it all!

HISTORIC SKYSCRAPERS

● The Home Insurance Building, built in Chicago in 1884, was the first tall building to be supported by a steel skeleton of columns and beams.

● New York's Empire State Building, opened in 1932, was the first building to have more than one hundred stories.

Bahrain World Trade Center's three wind turbines supply about 15 percent of its electricity.

Harnessing wind

The shape of the Bahrain World Trade Center is designed to make use of the wind, by directing it toward three wind turbines that hang from walkways connecting the two towers.

The Burj Khalifa, opened in 2010, holds the record for the tallest building in the world. It is 2,717 feet (828 m).

Hitting the Highway

Around a third of traffic accidents are caused by the road itself. Improvements in car design have cut down the number of road deaths, and now engineers are turning to technology to make roads safer, too.

Driverless cars

Driverless cars would reduce accidents.

Robot-controlled cars would be able to speed along while the owner reads the newspaper. Cars directed by GPS (the Global Positioning System) and loaded with sensors that "talk" with other cars' computers would need fewer safety features. As a result, they would be smaller and lighter and would use less fuel. Driverless cars are already legal in Nevada, and they could soon be appearing on a road near you.

Glow in the dark

Road markings on Dutch roads could soon be painted using a powder that absorbs sunlight and glows for up to ten hours overnight. Another new safety development is road markings painted with temperature-sensitive paint. When there is a risk of ice on the road, warning signals that look like snowflakes will appear.

Smart bridge

In 2007, the I-35W Mississippi River bridge collapsed, killing thirteen people. It was replaced by a "smart bridge" that warns computers of any small problems before they cause a disaster. The new bridge contains 323 sensors that monitor damage caused by traffic and Minnesota's freezing winters. Sensors in the road over the bridge automatically activate an anti-icing system when it is cold and watch out for damage.

💡 Know it all!

● Road surfaces made from solar panels could turn roads and pavements into a power source, reducing the number of power stations we need.

● These super-strong, high-tech road surfaces could heat themselves to melt ice and snow and could have built-in signs to warn drivers of danger ahead.

Going Green

As fuel prices rise, scientists are working hard to make transport more efficient so we can afford to keep on the move as well as save energy and reduce pollution.

Hybrid cars

Cars powered by gasoline or diesel can travel long distances between refueling, but they create a lot of pollution and are expensive to run. Electric cars produce almost no pollution but can go only about 100 miles (160 kilometers) before they need to be recharged. By combining a gas and an electric engine in one car, called a hybrid, drivers get the best of both worlds.

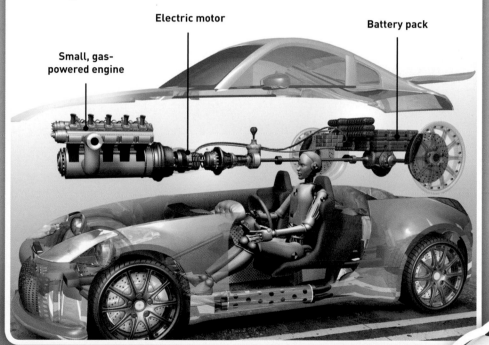

Small, gas-powered engine

Electric motor

Battery pack

Solar-powered boats

While electric hybrid cars are cutting greenhouse gases on land, solar-powered and hybrid boats are set to reduce carbon emissions at sea. The 102-foot-long (31-meter-long) *Tûranor PlanetSolar* is powered by 5,060 square feet (470 square meters) of solar panels. In May 2012, it became the first solar electric vehicle to travel all the way around the globe.

Getting the green light

Interactive street lights with motion sensors could reduce energy use by brightening as vehicles approach and switching off when the road is empty. The "wind light system" takes energy efficiency a step further. It uses tiny pinwheel generators, set into the edge of the road, to power the lights. As cars pass, the draft they create turns the pinwheels to generate electricity.

Electric cars could cut greenhouse gas emissions by 40 percent.

electric drive

Many street lights are already powered by solar technology.

The big picture!

Flying Without Wings

Imagine leaving New York City by train, traveling through a transatlantic tunnel, and arriving in London less than one hour later. Vacuum tube trains could change long-distance travel in the same way that airplanes did in the twentieth century.

Vactrains

The high-speed vactrain system would use maglev (short for magnetic levitation) trains running through airless tubes. Maglev trains float above a guideway, propelled by magnets. They can travel at more than 360 miles per hour (580 kilometers per hour), but if they operated in a vacuum tube, without air resistance or friction, they could reach supersonic speeds of more than 3,100 mph (5,000 kmh).

💡 Know it all!

● The first commercial maglev train started running between Shanghai city center and the airport in 2003

● A prototype maglev train has been unveiled in Japan—home to the famous bullet train. It will cut the bullet train's journey time in half and is due to open in 2027.

Know it all!

● Anyone who has played with magnets knows that opposite poles attract one another and identical poles push each other away. A maglev train has a set of large magnets attached to its underside, while a second set of magnets lines the guideway. These two sets of magnets repel one another so the train floats on a cushion of air 0.4 to 4 inches (1 to 10 centimeters) above the track. Power is then supplied to electromagnetic coils, which are constantly switched between alternating magnetic poles. These coils push and pull the train so it moves forward.

◈Flying by Wire

Most modern airliners are controlled by fly-by-wire technology, which was developed by **NASA**. The controls look similar to those in a standard cockpit, but their movements are changed to electronic signals, which are transmitted by computers.

Pilotless planes

In the future, passenger planes could be flown from a control room hundreds of miles away, using the same technology as unmanned drones. Drones (below) are already used for aerial photography and military missions.

The superjumbo

The double-decker Airbus 380 is 23 feet (73 m) in length, with a wingspan of 262 feet (80 m). The main parts of the plane are built in France, Germany, Spain, and the UK. Roads have been widened and special barges and canals have been built so the massive sections can be transported to the Airbus factory in Toulouse, France.

About a quarter of the plane's structure is made from lightweight, carbon-fiber reinforced plastic.

Parts of the A380 are made all over Europe and put together like a giant jigsaw puzzle at the factory in France.

F-22 Raptor

Modern fighters, such as the F-22 Raptor (below), combine stealth with technology. The plane's angular shape scatters radar beams, and its paint absorbs radar waves. A powerful onboard computer controls the fighter's radar, weapons, and flying systems, and a wireless link means pilots can share information without using the radio.

1. The **cockpit** is situated between the two passenger decks.

2. At take-off, the engines deliver a **thrust** equal to 3,500 car engines.

3. A **tail-mounted camera** gives passengers a bird's-eye view.

4. The main **computers** are located under the cockpit.

5. The plane carries between 555 and 853 **passengers**.

6. The cabin **lighting** changes from daylight to night to reduce jet lag.

7. The super-quiet **engines** mean there is less noise on board.

8. The A380 has twenty-two **wheels**—more than any other passenger aircraft.

Cruising at the Edge of Space

Suborbital vehicles fly at the boundary between Earth's atmosphere and outer space. At this height, air friction decreases, so aircraft can hit speeds of more than 3,100 mph (5,000 kmh).

Hypersonic flight

The Concorde was the first supersonic civilian aircraft. When it was scrapped in 2003, supersonic air travel became a thing of the past. Now a British company is developing an engine that could make it possible to fly from Europe to Australia in four hours. It would use a turbojet, like the Concorde's, to reach supersonic speeds—then it would switch to rocket mode, taking the aircraft to Mach 6 and above as it flies at the edge of space.

The Concorde had to take off and land at a steep angle because of its delta wings, so designers gave it a nose that could be lowered to give the pilot a clear view of the runway.

> ### Know it all!
>
> ● In 1947, American pilot Chuck Yeager became the first person to fly faster than the speed of sound (Mach 1).
>
> ● In 1962, the X-15 reached a speed of Mach 6.7—four times faster than a speeding bullet.

WhiteKnightTwo has twin fuselages that are identical to SpaceShipTwo. SpaceShipTwo hangs between them as it is carried up to 9.3 miles (15,000 m).

SpaceShipTwo on display at the Farnborough Air Show, UK.

SpaceShipTwo

More than 530 passengers have booked their place in space aboard Virgin Galactic's suborbital craft, which broke apart during a test flight in 2014. It consists of two parts—SpaceShipTwo, which has room for six passengers, and the WhiteKnightTwo transporter. WhiteKnightTwo takes off from a normal runway and carries SpaceShipTwo to an altitude of 9.3 miles (15,000 m). Then SpaceShipTwo breaks free, fires its boosters, and soars to a height of 68 miles (110,000 m).

Nanotechnology

Imagine a world so tiny that everything is measured in millionths of a millimeter. "Nano" means "billionth," so a nanometer is one billionth of a meter. Nanotechnology could transform our lives during the twenty-first century.

Nanorobots

Nanorobots could be programmed to make anything from diamonds to food. Instead of processing materials to make things, nanorobots would build them atom by atom, as nature does. By building products directly from atoms and molecules, goods could be produced cheaply without any waste.

Nanorobots would make copies of themselves until there were enough to begin production.

Facts & figures!

MICRO MEASUREMENTS

● One nanometer is the length your fingernail grows in a second.

● An atom measures between 0.1 and 0.5 of a nanometer.

● A computer transistor is 100 to 200 nanometers wide.

● A human hair is between 60,000 and 100,000 nanometers in diameter.

Nanotechnology today

Nanotechnologists' ideas sound like science fiction, but nanotechnology is already part of our lives. Stain-resistant fabrics are coated with "nanowhiskers," while some cosmetics and sunscreens contain nanoscopic materials. Nano-coatings are found on self-cleaning glass, and some tennis balls have an interior coating of clay nanoparticles to stop air from escaping from them.

Dream or nightmare?

Nanorobots could change our lives for the better, but some people are worried that nanoparticles could poison us or be dangerous for wildlife. Another theory, called the "grey goo scenario," suggests that nanomachines could get out of control and reproduce so fast that they would strip Earth of everything, leaving a lifeless planet inhabited by nothing but nanorobots.

Nanomaterials

The latest nanomaterials could be used to produce paper-thin televisions that can be rolled up and a computer you can fold and put in your pocket.

Graphene

In 2004, physicists discovered an almost invisible material, called graphene, that is two hundred times stronger than steel and tougher than a diamond. It stretches like rubber, conducts heat and electricity better than copper, and is almost weightless. A sheet of graphene is just one atom thick, and a 0.04-inch-high (1-millimeter-high) pile of it would contain three million sheets. In the future, graphene will allow us to create superfast phones and paper-thin computers.

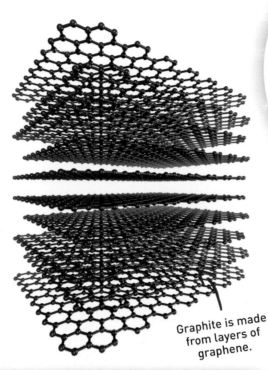

Graphite is made from layers of graphene.

Quantum dots can produce any color in the spectrum.

Quantum dots

Quantum dots could soon be found in everything from energy-saving lightbulbs to phones, TVs, and movie screens. When they are activated, these fluorescent crystals glow a particular color depending on their size and the material used. Today's LED screens show only about 30 percent of the colors our eyes can see, but groups of quantum dots will produce bright bursts of light in a full range of colors.

Carbon nanotubes

If a sheet of carbon atoms is rolled into a cylinder, it forms a carbon nanotube that is a hundred times stronger than steel, but six times lighter. Nanotubes are already being used to make tennis rackets and golf clubs lighter and stronger, and engineers are working on ways to incorporate them into cars and planes.

Scientists have found a way to spin carbon nanotubes into superstrong thread, finer than human hair.

Glue made from carbon nanotubes is modeled on geckos' feet, so one day we might be able to strap on nanotube shoes and walk up walls like Spiderman.

💡 Know it all!

● Carbon nanotubes could be made into an ultra-lightweight rope, strong enough to support a "space elevator" to shuttle cargo and people into orbit.

⬛ Generating Electricity

Electricity is often seen as clean energy. Electric cars are called "green," for example. However, many power stations burn coal, oil, or gas, which release greenhouse gases, to produce electricity.

Power stations

Thomas Edison built one of the first power stations in New York in 1882. Until then, energy had to be produced where it was needed, but a power station made it possible to generate electricity in Arizona that would be used in California. Most power stations produce electricity by burning fuel to create steam (see the panel on the right). Whichever fuel is used, the basic process is the same.

Power cables supported by pylons carry the electricity to where it is needed.

The steam turbine at a power plant

💡 Know it all!

● Electricity is usually produced by burning fuel in a furnace.

● Heat from the furnace flows around pipes full of cold water. The heat boils the water and turns it into steam.

● The high-pressure steam turns the blades of a turbine.

● The turbine is linked to a generator, which uses the energy from the turbine to make electricity.

Nuclear power

Nuclear reactors heat water by splitting an atom of enriched uranium into two. The uranium is formed into pellets, put in metal tubes, and lowered into water inside a reactor. There the atoms are split, releasing huge amounts of energy. Nuclear power stations produce very clean energy, but uranium gives off radiation, which can be dangerous in high doses.

Renewable Energy

Coal, oil, and natural gas are fossil fuels. They produce greenhouse gases when they are burned, and they will run out one day, so scientists are looking for clean, renewable sources of energy instead.

Biofuel

Biofuels are made from plants and produce fewer air pollutants than fossil fuels do. Ethanol made from grains, sugar cane, or potato skins can be mixed with gasoline, while biodiesel made from vegetable oil is used in diesel engines. Biofuels are a sustainable source of energy but they are made from crops that could be eaten.

Wind power

In power stations, turbines are moved by steam and their energy is transferred to a generator. Wind turbines produce electricity in the same way, using the wind instead of steam. The generator in a wind turbine is in the horizontal shaft that is attached to the blades.

Solar energy

Sunlight is made up of photons, or particles of solar energy. When photons strike a photovoltaic cell, some are absorbed. These photons knock electrons loose from the cell's material, and the electrons can then flow around a circuit, producing an electrical current.

Wind farms are often built offshore because there is more wind out at sea.

Sunflower seeds can be used to make biodiesel.

A field of solar panels provides more energy than the same field planted with a biofuel crop.

Hydroelectric power

The Three Gorges Dam, which spans China's Yangtze River, is the world's largest hydropower station. Water from the reservoir behind the 1.4-mile (2.3 km) dam surges through large pipes that lead to thirty-two turbines. These are connected to generators that produce 10 percent of China's electricity—equivalent to eleven nuclear power stations.

Biotechnology

Biotechnology uses biology to make new products. If you have eaten bread or yogurt, you have consumed foods that were developed using biotechnology.

History of biotechnology

Biotechnology began thousands of years ago when people started using microbes to produce wine, bread, and cheese. Later, when corn and potatoes were introduced from the Americas in the sixteenth century, European farmers bred varieties that were suited to their local growing conditions. More recently, fruit and vegetable plants were cross-fertilized to produce better crops.

Bacteria are used to change milk into yogurt. This is an example of biotechnology.

Selective breeding

Selective breeding is a form of biotechnology. Over the centuries, humans have bred plants and animals that have particular characteristics by choosing their parents carefully. These include cows that give more milk, potatoes that are resistant to disease, and flowers that have the best color or scent. Dogs once looked very similar, and it is due to selective breeding that we now have so many different types.

Other uses

Biotechnology is used to make medicines and to detect and treat genetic health problems. In industry, biotechnology is used to produce biofuels and biodegradable plastics that reduce our use of fossil fuels. Bioplastics are made from starchy crops, including corn, sugar cane, and wheat.

Selective breeding has created dogs of all shapes and sizes.

Hot shots!

★ SLICK SOLUTION

When the *Deepwater Horizon* oil rig exploded in 2010, underwater bacteria gobbled up tons of oil. Now, biotechnologists are growing these bacteria to help clean up oil following a spill.

Genetic Engineering

Genetic engineering is a type of biotechnology. Traditional breeding methods mix many genes from the same species together, but genetic engineering allows a single gene to be changed. This means, for example, that a gene from a jellyfish can be added to the DNA of a pig to produce a piglet that glows in the dark.

Know it all!

● The first GM food for sale to the public was a tomato developed in 1994.

Genetic modification can make crops more resistant to drought.

The GM battlefield

Genetic modification (GM) is another name for genetic engineering. Not everyone agrees about whether or not genetic modification is a good thing.

By adding a gene from disease-resistant wild plants, the use of chemicals could be reduced.

Pro GM

People who support GM think that it is an improvement on selective breeding. GM crops can produce more food and use less land, water, fertilizer, and pesticides. This could help people in the developing world who rely on crops such as cassava, corn, and rice as their main sources of food. Apart from increasing the harvest, foods could be modified by adding vitamins and minerals to make them more nutritious.

This picture is not real, but it illustrates the idea that genetic modification can combine genes from two different organisms.

Against GM

Those who are against GM say that genetically engineered crops could harm other plants. It is not known how GM plants would affect wildlife, and if genes from different foods are mixed together, this could be dangerous for people with allergies. Many GM crops are not affected by weed killers, so farmers can spray whole fields with herbicides. GM protestors claim that, instead of reducing the use of chemicals, GM crops will increase it.

Bees could transfer pollen from GM crops to organic plants growing nearby.

Future Foods

By 2050, the world's population will have grown to nine billion, and scientists are trying to find new ways to feed the extra two billion people. The answer could be a diet that includes insects, algae, and meat grown in a lab.

Dutch scientists have already produced the first test-tube burger.

This tasty Thai plateful of insects is rich in protein.

Seaweed is a very nutritious food.

Bug burger, anyone?

At least 1,400 insect species are eaten in Africa, Asia, and South America. These low-fat minibeasts are rich in protein, and insect farms use a fraction of the energy needed to produce other meats. Some people may not be keen to eat creepy crawlies, so scientists are looking into ways of extracting their protein for use in sausages and patties.

Manufactured meat

Worldwide, people eat about 275.6 million tons (250 million t) of meat each year, and this could double by 2050. Rearing animals for meat uses a lot of land and water, so scientists are developing artificial meat. It may be many years before we are eating a lab-grown leg of lamb, but an artificial hamburger has recently been produced by Dutch scientists.

Super seaweed

Seaweed is rich in nutrients, low in fat, and good for us. It is good for the environment, too. Seaweed absorbs carbon dioxide and produces oxygen, and it does not use up valuable land space or fresh water. Many people are already eating seaweed, or algae; carrageenan and agar, which are used to thicken processed foods, are both made from algae.

Farming

A shortage of farmland could threaten the world's food supply as the population grows, so scientists are thinking of growing crops in places where farming was thought to be impossible, such as deserts and city centers.

Vertical farming

Food producers are considering growing crops in skyscraper greenhouses right in the center of cities. Seeds would be sown in trays on the top floor and fed with water and nutrients as they move down the building on a conveyer belt. By the time they reach the bottom they would be ready for harvesting.

Seawater greenhouses

Crops could be grown in deserts near the coast in greenhouses that convert seawater to fresh water. Seawater evaporators, powered by solar energy, turn seawater into cool water vapor, which is then pumped into the greenhouse. The water vapor condenses (like steamy air on a cold window), and this fresh water is used to irrigate (water) the crops.

Future farmhands

Modern farmers already rely on technology to save time and money. There are robots that milk cows, machines that harvest soft fruits, and tractors that sow seeds and apply fertilizer with tenths-of-an-inch precision. Now robots with octopus-like arms may take on the job of picking tree fruits, such as apples.

Seawater greenhouses could turn deserts into fertile land.

The greenhouse would have its own bees and other helpful insects.

💡 Know it all!

● Fields could be seeded with microbes that pull nitrogen from the air, reducing the need for nitrogen fertilizers.

● Infrared light will be used to show exactly where there are weeds, reducing the amount of weed killer needed.

● Soil sensors could calculate how much fertilizer and water crops need and send the information directly to the farmer's computer.

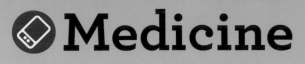Medicine

In the past, scientists suggested that people could never survive beyond the age of 120, but new technologies could increase our lifespans by repairing damaged cells and providing us with replacement organs when our bodies start to wear out.

Stem cells may be able to create new organs, regrow damaged spinal cords, or cure many diseases in years to come.

A nanorobot injects drugs into a red blood cell.

Nanomedicine

Nanotechnology could transform medicine and surgery by treating everything from heart disease to cancer using nanorobots the size of bacteria. Nanomachines could be injected into the body to deliver drugs to the site of an infection, kill cancer cells, or perform surgery. One day, scientists may even be able to grow new body parts using nanotechnology.

Gene therapy

Gene therapy is an exciting new field of medical research that uses genes to treat or prevent disease. It could replace a bad gene that causes disease with a healthy copy, turn off a bad gene, or introduce a new gene into the body to fight a disease.

Genes are short sections of DNA. A person's DNA is recorded as a sequence of the letters A, T, G, and C.

Stem cell technology

Stem cells are special because they can develop into different types of cells and can renew themselves many times. Embryonic stem cells come from unborn babies and can grow into any of the two hundred cell types in the body. Adult stem cells are found in body tissues and have been altered by scientists to create other types of cells. Many diseases, including Alzheimer's and diabetes, might be cured by stem cell technology. Stem cells could also be used to grow replacement organs.

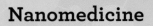

Bionic Body Parts

Today's most advanced bionic limbs are intelligent, robotic machines that respond to their user's nerve and muscle signals. They "think" like real body parts—legs automatically adjust the angle of the toe or lock the knee, for example.

Bionic arm

The latest bionic arms are controlled by thought, just like a real arm. Surgeons rewire the patient's nervous system so the nerves that previously moved the missing arm are transferred to the chest. A computer processes the electrical signals from the nerves and instructs the bionic arm to perform the movement.

Bionic leg

Electronic sensors in the leg keep track of its position and changes in weight on the knee, ankle, and foot. Processors then decide how best to respond and make the necessary adjustments.

The artificial knee joint moves like a real knee.

The leg is moved by hydraulic components.

Sensors send messages about the angle of the leg and how much weight is being put on it so that the limb can work out what will happen next and react accordingly.

The brain sends a message to the missing arm via the nerves, just as if it were still there.

The nerves that would normally be connected to the missing arm are moved to the chest, where electrodes pick up the nerves' messages and pass them to the bionic arm's computer as electrical signals.

Know it all!

● Powered exoskeletons can help some paralyzed people to walk or move about.

● Bionic eye implants convert light into electrical impulses that are sent to the brain.

● Artificial pancreases and kidneys should soon be available.

Glossary

Atom The smallest particle of an element that can exist.

Biometric The measurement of unique personal features, such as fingerprints.

Bionic Artificial, electronic body parts.

Carbon One of the most common elements.

Carbon emissions The release of carbon dioxide into the air through the burning of fossil fuels.

Cell The smallest unit of an organism. We have more than two hundred types of cells.

Chip (computer) A small electrical circuit used to process information.

Data (computer) Information stored or processed by a computer.

DNA Deoxyribonucleic acid (DNA) looks like a twisted ladder and is found within our cells. It can be compared to a list of instructions that tells the cell what to do.

Drone An aircraft without a pilot, controlled from the ground or from another plane.

Electron A tiny particle that forms part of every atom and carries electricity.

Exoskeleton A skeleton that is outside the body. Powered exoskeletons are like frames that help people to walk.

Fiber-optic cable A cable, made up of strands of pure glass as thin as a human hair, that carries digital information.

Fossil fuels Fuels such as oil, coal, or gas that have formed over millions of years from the remains of prehistoric plants and animals.

Genes Sections of DNA that are passed on from parent to offspring.

GPS The Global Positioning System (GPS) is made up of a number of satellites that work together to pinpoint an exact location on Earth.

Graphite A soft, black form of carbon that is used in lead pencils.

Greenhouse gases Gases in the atmosphere, including water vapor, carbon dioxide, nitrous oxide and methane, that trap energy from the sun. Scientists think that human activities, such as burning fossil fuels, are increasing greenhouse gases and making Earth warmer.

Hybrid Something made by combining two different things or species.

Hydraulic Hydraulic systems transfer force from one place to another by applying pressure to a liquid, such as oil.

Irrigate To water (plants, for example).

LED Light-emitting diode. When LEDs are connected to an electrical current, the electrons within the diode release photons, which we see as light.

Mach The speed of sound (761 mph or 1,225 kmh). Mach 2 is twice the speed of sound, for example.

Microbe A microorganism, particularly a bacterium.

Neural network A computer system modeled on the brain and nervous system.

Organism An animal, plant, or single-celled life form.

Printed circuit board A thin board "printed" with electrical wires that connect the electronic parts in a computer, smartphone, TV, etc.

QR code A quick-response barcode that can be scanned by the camera in a smartphone and is linked to a website or telephone number.

Radar Radar detects the position, movement, and nature of an object by tracking the radio waves reflected from its surface.

Silicon Silicon is a common chemical element. Sand and glass both contain silicon, and very pure silicon is the basis for modern computer chips.

Smartphone A smartphone combines a mobile phone with computer technology.

Stem cells Cells that can renew themselves many times by dividing. Stem cells can be grown and transformed into specialized cells.

Transistor A switch that is used to control the flow of electricity in electronic equipment.

Turbine A machine that produces energy when a wheel is made to turn by a fast-moving flow of water, steam, or gas.

Uranium A radioactive metal used as a fuel in nuclear reactors.

Further Information

BOOKS

Cook, David. *Robot Building for Beginners*, 2nd edition. Technology in Action. New York: Apress, 2010.

Beyer, Mark. *Transportation of the Future*. High Interest Books. New York: Children's Press, 2002.

McPartland, Randall. *Understanding the Laws of Thermodynamics*. Mastering Physics. New York: Cavendish Square Publishing, 2015.

Sullivan, Laura L. *The Pros and Cons of Solar Power*. Economics of Energy. New York: Cavendish Square Publishing, 2014.

WEBSITES

Discover – Tech

news.discovery.com/tech

Discovery Communications provides news articles and videos on the latest in technology, and provides information on the newest gear and gadgets.

Popular Science

www.popsci.com/tags/technology

Stay up to date with the latest news on the rapidly changing world of technology from the editors of this informative magazine.

Index

Page numbers in **boldface** are illustrations. Entries in **boldface** are glossary terms.

Airbus 380, 16, **16**
aircraft, 16–17, **16**, **17**
appliances, smart, 10, **10**
artificial intelligence, 8–9
artificial neural network, 8
atoms, 18–20

Bahrain World Trade Center, 11, **11**
Berners-Lee, Tim, 5
biofuel, 21, 22
biometric door locks, 10, **10**
bionic body parts, 27, **27**
biotechnology, 22–23
bits and bytes, 6
bridge, "smart," 12, **12**
Burj Khalifa, 11, **11**

Cailliau, Robert, 5
carbon, 13, 19
carbon emissions, 13
cars, 12–13, **12**, **13**, 20
cells, 26
chips, 6–7
cloud computing, 5
computers, 4–8, **6**
   in aircraft, 16
   in cars, 12
   farming and, 25
   home automation systems, 10
   in roads and bridges, 12
   in robots, 9

Concorde, 17, **17**
CPU, 6, **6**
crops, 22–25, **23**

data, 4
Deepwater Horizon oil rig, 22
DNA, 23
drones, 16, **16**

Edison, Thomas, 20
electricity, 13, 20–21
electrons, 21
email, 4, 5
exoskeleton, 27

farming, 23–25
fiber-optic cables, 4, **4**
food, 24–25
fossil fuels, 21–22
F-22 Raptor, 16, **16**

genes, 23, 26
gene therapy, 26
genetic engineering, 23
GPS, 12
graphene, 19, **19**
graphite, 19, **19**
greenhouse gases, 13, 20–21

Heliotrope home, 10, **10**
homes, high-tech, 10
hybrid cars, 13, **13**
hydraulics, 27
hydroelectric power, 21

insects, consumption of, 24, **24**
Internet, 4–5, 7
irrigation, 25

laptops, 6–7, **6**
LED, **6**, 19

Mach speed, 17
maglev trains, 14–15, **14–15**
magnets, 14–15
meat, artificial, 24
medicine, 22, 26–27
microbes, 22, 25
Moore's law, 7
motherboard, 6, **6**

nanomaterials, 19
nanomedicine, 26
nanorobots, 18, **18**, 26, **26**
nanotechnology, 7, 18–19, 26
nanotubes, carbon, 19, **19**
NASA, 9, 16
neural network, 8
nuclear power, 20, **20**

organism, 23

packets, 4, **4**
power stations, 20–21, **20**
printed circuit board, 6

QR codes, 5, **5**
quantum dots, 19

radar, 16
renewable energy, 21
roads, improvements to, 12–13, **12**

robots, 8–9, **8**, **9**
   on farms, 25
   industrial, 9
   nanorobots, 18
   robot pets, 9, **9**
   snake robots, 9
   vacuum cleaners, 9, **9**

seawater greenhouses, 25
seaweed, 24, **24**
selective breeding, 22–23
silicon, 6–7
skyscrapers, 11, 25
smartphones, 5, **5**, 10
social networking, 5
solar power, 10, 12–13, **13**, 21, **21**, 25
SpaceShipTwo, 17, **17**
stem cells, 26, **26**
suborbital vehicles, 17

tablets, 6–7, 7
Taipei 101, 11, **11**
Three Gorges Dam, 21, 21
trains, 14–15
transistors, 6–7, 18
tuned mass damper, 11, **11**
Tûranor PlanetSolar, 13, **13**
turbines, 11, 20–21, **20**
Turing test, 8

uranium, 20

vactrain system, 14–15, **14–15**

wind power, 11, 13, 21, **21**
World Wide Web, 5

Yeager, Chuck, 17